Published by
Hasmark Publishing International
www.hasmarkpublishing.com

Disclaimer
This book is designed to provide information and motivation to our readers. It is sold with the understanding that the publisher is not engaged to render any type of psychological, legal, or any other kind of professional advice. The content of each article is the sole expression and opinion of its author, and not necessarily that of the publisher. No warranties or guarantees are expressed or implied by the publisher's choice to include any of the content in this volume. Neither the publisher nor the individual author(s) shall be liable for any physical, psychological, emotional, financial, or commercial damages, including, but not limited to, special, incidental, consequential or other damages. Our views and rights are the same: You are responsible for your own choices, actions, and results.

Editor: Allison Burney
allison.burney@gmail.com

Book Layout: Anne Karklins
anne@hasmarkpublishing.com

ISBN 13: 978-1-989756-28-7
ISBN 10: 198975628X

"This beautifully illustrated children's book is based on a fascinating idea that explores heaven and earth"

    – **Peggy McColl**, *New York Times* Bestselling Author

"Have you ever wondered how children feel when they don't expect something? **The Loneliest Teddy Bear** *is a heartwarming story about hope, intuition and courage. Shaaron Fedora's beautiful writing is a testament to how resilient we all are as human beings, especially children. This book will make you smile, cry and give you that glimmer of magic that we all crave. A MUST have story for every family!"*

    – **Judy O'Beirn**, Hasmark Publishing International, Founder & President,
      International Bestselling Author of *Unwavering Strength Series*

*"***The Loneliest Teddy Bear** *is a book that encompasses hope. This story is about resolution and finding the inner child in all of us. Shaaron writes with beautiful precision as the illustrations bring storytelling to life. I recommend that every family utilises this book as a tool for courage. A wonderful story that will pull on your heartstrings."*

    – **Pashmina P.**, International Bestselling Author of *What is a Gupsey?* and
      The Cappuccino Chronicles Trilogy

THE LONELIEST TEDDYBEAR

Written by Shaaron Fedora   Illustrated by Kezzia Crossley

Hasmark
PUBLISHING
INTERNATIONAL

For all the Teddy Bears of the world,
who love or are loved by a Person.

We met in Heaven in that time between lives.

THE PLAN

We met in Heaven in that time between lives.
We, meaning me and my Person.

We spent all our days together
and grew to love each other very much.
Our love was enormous.
It spilled out into the universe
and fell like stardust upon the Earth.

When the time came to choose our next life,
together, me and my Person made a grand plan.
Our plan was to meet up on Earth and
continue our joyous friendship there.

We knew it would be challenging,
because my Person planned to be born here,
and I planned to go to a factory in Bangladesh.

It was a complicated plan with many twists and turns,
across many miles and halfway around the world.

In Heaven, all things are possible.

But we were in Heaven
where all things are possible.
We trusted the Universe to work out the details.

On Earth, such details are called coincidences.
In Heaven, we know there are no coincidences.
There's only the miraculous workings
of the intricate plan of life.

Nothing is accidental.
Everything has a purpose.

Every person you meet, every single one,
is part of the plan.
Some stay in our lives for only a moment.
There might only be time for a glance and a smile.

But then there are others, like me and my Person –
others who are destined to be part of your forever.

Me and my Person set out for Planet Earth.

As soon as our plan was completed,
me and my Person set out for Planet Earth.

And just like everyone who comes to Earth,
as soon as we got here,
we forgot the plan.

That seems to be the way it goes.
Life gets in the way.

But every now and then, something happens.
A memory flashes before my eyes,
so briefly I can't quite get hold of it.

It's there. Then - poof - it's gone.

But it reminds me
that somewhere, there is a plan.
It lets me know that I am on my path.

Teddy bears aren't any more alike than people are.

THE SHELF

Until I was chosen,
I was just like any other bear
sitting on a shelf in the toy department.

Now, I don't mean to say that all bears
on the shelf were just like me.
I don't mean that at all.

Teddy bears aren't any more alike than people are.

Some of us are playful with playful personalities,
while others are more serious.
Some of us would be considered cute,
and some of us are handsome and dignified, like me.
We come in all sizes,
from rather small bears to the gigantic teddy bears,
like the ones you see at the fair.

I, myself, am middle sized, not too small, not too large.

Once you're on the shelf, you strive to be noticed.

Like people, we come in many colors.
And, like people, some of us have deep blue eyes, like mine.
Some have smoldering dark eyes,
so dark as to be called black.
And, of course, most bears have brown eyes,
just like most people.

The one thing (and maybe the only thing)
that is the same for all of us is this:

Every teddy bear, that is now or ever will be,
has the quiescent gift
of loving and being loved by a person.

To be loved by a person is the greatest gift of all.
But first, one has to be chosen,
and that's the purpose of the shelf.

Once you're on the shelf, you strive to be noticed.
It's important to set yourself apart.

When they look into my eyes, they will know who I am.

I resolved to be the most loving of all teddy bears,
so that when the right person came by
and looked deep into my eyes,
they would know who I was.

I knew my purpose and
I knew there was a plan of sorts.

For sure, me and my Person had not worked out the details.
One can't do much of that ahead of time anyway,
because every person has free will
which must be honored.

Even though I had forgotten a lot about our plan,
I knew who I was and I trusted the Universe.

I knew that I was capable of deep and lasting love,
that I was trustworthy and reliable, and
that I was strong enough to take on whatever life gave me.

I knew I would be there for my Person
now and forever.

All teddy bears yearn to belong to a person.

As Teddy Bears, we promise to be there for our Person,
to celebrate the good times and the good days,
and to give comfort on bad days.

We know going in that that is the deal.
We accept this fully, without reservation.
Otherwise, we don't get to be chosen.
We don't get to be real.

Loving and comforting one person is our reason for being.

All teddy bears have an innate yearning
to belong to a person,
and until we are chosen,
there is a lonely, empty space within us,
waiting and wanting.

I was very happy to be there on the shelf,
waiting,
letting the world know of the love I had to share.

Bands should play and people should march in the streets.

BECOMING REAL

And then I was chosen!

Ah, the moment we are chosen
- that sweet, sweet moment -
when we become real.

That is the moment
when we and our person
become inextricably bonded,
now and forever and on into eternity.

It is an auspicious moment.

Time should really stand still.
Bands should play and people should march in the streets.
Earth should stop turning for this one moment,
just long enough for the world to sit up and take notice,
to shout,
"LOVE IS HAPPENING HERE!"

I just didn't know it would feel like this.

The world needs to be reminded
of how awesome it is that a Person has been given
unconditional love and comfort for all their days.

I had been told, over and over again, about this moment,
the moment I would be chosen.

I knew what would happen.
I just didn't know it would feel like this.

How my heart would beat so fast and so loudly,
like it was trying to jump out of my stuffed body.
How it would grow so fast and so large
there would hardly be enough room for it.

It was overwhelming.
I needed a moment to steady myself,
to be still.

For the first time, I felt it fully.
I felt the enormity of what I was about to undertake,
the grave importance of it.

...to celebrate the joy of my Person's life.

THE PROMISE

I was to be comfort for my Person forever.

That is no small thing.
Loving a Person unconditionally,
forever,
is about the most important thing in the world.

I promised
to be there always, with and for my Person,
to celebrate the joy of my Person's life and
to comfort my Person in every sorrow
that might come to pass.

I promised this
for always and forever.

We had found each other!

"Me and my Person,
        my Person and me!
Me and my Person,
        my Person and me!"

I sang these words over and over again, right out loud,
as I danced about the room.

I loved the sound of it.
Even more, I loved the feel of it.

We had found each other!

It was just like we planned.
And now, we would be together
for the rest of our lives.

What is a Teddy Bear
without a Person?

AND THEN

I know I'm rather vague about the plan we made,
but I know this much.

We planned to find each other here on Earth.
And we did.

We planned to stay together to the end of our days.
And we did.

I just didn't know my Person would leave so soon.
I don't remember that being part of the plan.

My Person has gone, and I am alone.
And what is a Teddy Bear without a Person?

I don't know how to go on alone. I don't know how to do it.

But I must find a way.
I must find a way, because that's the way Teddy Bears love.

I am the loneliest Teddy Bear in the World.

We don't quit.
We don't quit, no matter how hard it is.
We don't quit, no matter how much it hurts.

We keep our promise.

Sometimes people say the most useless things.
Someone said I would get over it,
but I won't.

Teddy Bears have only one Person,
and my Person is gone.

People say there will be others.
Don't they know, it doesn't matter if there are others?
It doesn't matter if there are a million others.
My Person is gone.

And I am the loneliest Teddy Bear in the world.

Someday, the rain will stop.

I know what has happened.

I know my Person has gone home to Heaven,
and I know
that someday I, too, will go home.

I know that my Person is being
cared for and loved
by angels,
whose special grace is to love and care
for all the children who go home
before their parents.

I know all that.

But I miss my Person.

HOW TO USE THIS BOOK

Give this book, along with a teddy bear, to a child who has lost someone –
a friend, a sibling, a parent or grandparent.

The teddy bear should be large enough (the bigger, the better)
so the child can hold the bear in their arms
and give the bear a real "bear hug."

The Teddy Bear and the Person in the story made their plan to
be together before they came to Earth. Even though they had forgotten
the details of their plan (we all do), they knew there was a plan.

You might suggest to the child that the person who has left also had a plan,
and loving the child was an important part of that plan.
Remind them that the one who has gone will miss us, just as we miss them.
And remind them that one day, we will meet again.

Children, with their natural empathy, will attempt to comfort the lonely
Teddy Bear with soft words and "bear hugs."

In turn and in time, the Teddy Bear will comfort the child.

Other books by Shaaron Fedora:

PIPPA & Her Guardian Angel
JEMMA The Most Wondering Angel
Twigs In My Ears

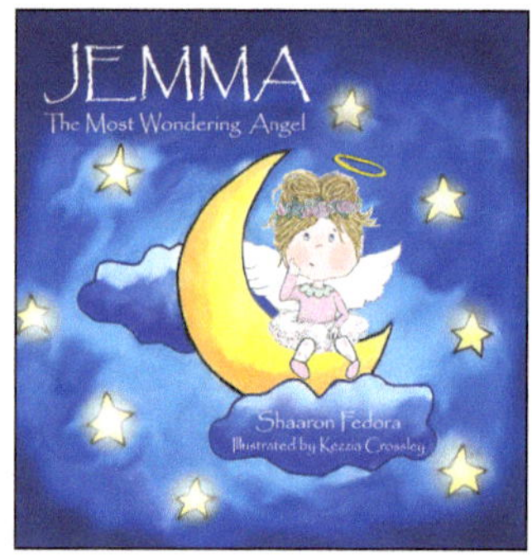

Contact Information
https://shaaronfedora.com/
Facebook.com/ShaaronFedoraAuthor

About the Author

Born in Saskatoon, Saskatchewan, Shaaron spent her early years on her parents' farm, moving to the city for high school. Shaaron was part of a large, close-knit family, and as adults, family and friends became synonymous. Shaaron is the mother of five (4 daughters & 1 son), a grandmother and a GG (GG stands for great-grandmother, but she prefers GG).

Shaaron is a writer, an author, a crafter, a designer/decorator, and a home renovator. She appreciates beauty in all its manifestations, including the beauty of order.

Her stories reflect the spiritual aspect of the human condition. They are gentle stories giving children a feeling of being safe in the world. They convey the message to children and adults alike that our lives have purpose. They are part of a plan that we helped design. Shaaron is now retired and lives in Coquitlam, BC.

With every donation, a voice will be given to
the creativity that lies within the hearts of
our children living with diverse challenges.

By making this difference, children that may
not have been given the opportunity to have their
Heart Heard will have the freedom to create
beautiful works of art and musical creations.

Donate by visiting

HeartstobeHeard.com

We thank you.